TABLE OF CONTENTS

BIG GUY, BIG HITTER

On October 4, 2022, Aaron Judge made **American League** history. He hit his 62nd home run of the season.

A Crabtree Branches Book

Today's Stars

AARON JUDGE

Samantha Bell

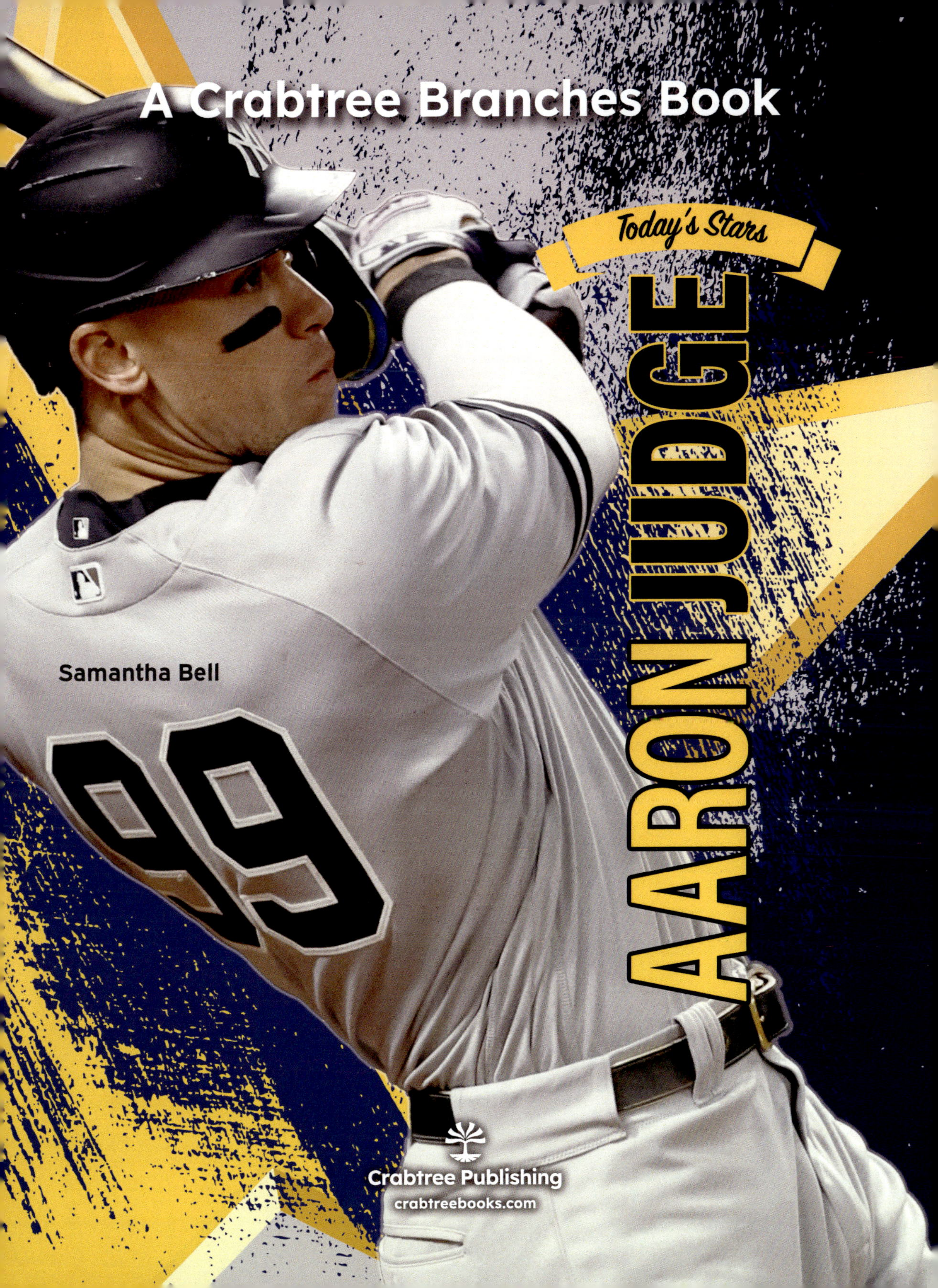

Crabtree Publishing
crabtreebooks.com

School-to-Home Support for Caregivers and Teachers

This high-interest book is designed to motivate striving students with engaging topics while building fluency, vocabulary, and an interest in reading. Here are a few questions and activities to help the reader build upon his or her comprehension skills.

Before Reading:

- *What do I think this book is about?*
- *What do I know about this topic?*
- *What do I want to learn about this topic?*
- *Why am I reading this book?*

During Reading:

- *I wonder why...*
- *I'm curious to know...*
- *How is this like something I already know?*
- *What have I learned so far?*

After Reading:

- *What was the author trying to teach me?*
- *What are some details?*
- *How did the photographs and captions help me understand more?*
- *Read the book again and look for the vocabulary words.*
- *What questions do I still have?*

Extension Activities:

- *What was your favorite part of the book? Write a paragraph on it.*
- *Draw a picture of your favorite thing you learned from the book.*

Aaron is an **outfielder** for the New York Yankees. But Aaron is more than just a great athlete. He is a team player. His coaches and teammates **respect** him. In December 2022, he was named team captain. Now he is officially leading the team.

Fun Facts

Aaron is 6 feet, 7 inches (2 m) tall and weighs 282 pounds (128 kg). He is nearly 6 inches (15 cm) taller and 70 pounds (32 kg) heavier than the average-sized baseball player.

LOTS OF SUPPORT

Aaron Judge was born on April 26, 1992. He was adopted by Patty and Wayne Judge, who are both teachers. His parents are white, and Aaron is **biracial**. He has an older brother named John, who is also adopted.

Aaron poses for a photo with his wife, Samantha, and parents, Patty and Wayne, after a press conference at Yankee Stadium in New York on December 21, 2022.

Aaron grew up in a small **agricultural** town called Linden in California. As a boy, he played first base and pitcher in Little League. He was the biggest player on his team.

Fun Facts

Aaron credits his mom with his success. He said she taught him to know the difference between right and wrong, how to treat people, and how to put in extra work.

ALL-AROUND ATHLETE

By the time he got to high school, Aaron was already 6 feet (1.8 m) tall. He played on his high school's baseball, basketball, and football teams.

Aaron worked hard at all three sports. He set the record for his school for touchdowns as a wide receiver in football. He scored 18.2 points per game as a basketball center. In baseball, he hit a total of 11 home runs over three years.

Fun Facts

Throughout high school, Aaron played sports just because he enjoyed it. Near the end of each sport's season, he would be tired of playing that sport and look forward to the next one.

COLLEGE DAYS

After high school, Aaron was a 31st-round pick by the Oakland Athletics **professional** baseball team. He had to choose between becoming a professional baseball player or going to college. Growing up in a family of teachers helped him decide to go to college.

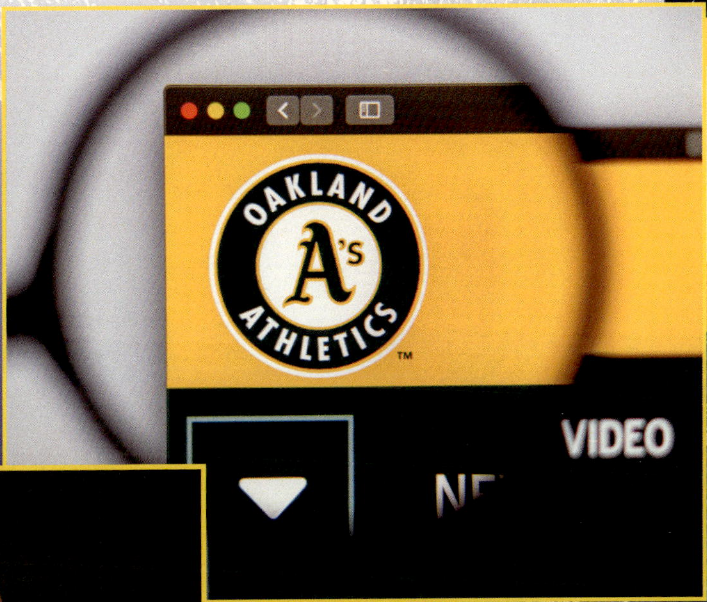

Many universities offered Aaron **scholarships** to play football. But Aaron decided to focus on baseball instead.

EASTON

Aaron accepted a pitching scholarship from Fresno State University. While playing on the Fresno State Bulldogs baseball team, he practiced hard, improved a lot, and won many awards.

Aaron hits a single with the Fresno State Bulldogs during an NCAA baseball game on May 4, 2013.

Fun Facts

Aaron helped lead Fresno State to the 2011 and 2012 College World Series.

GOING PRO

During Aaron's time with the Fresno State Bulldogs, baseball **scouts** were impressed with his performance. In the first round of the 2013 **draft**, Aaron was the second player picked by the New York Yankees. He was going to play on one of the Yankees' minor league teams. But because of a torn muscle, he sat out much of the 2013 season.

Aaron throws a ball back to a fan on May 21, 2015, after a win with the Trenton Thunder.

Aaron went on to play the next two seasons with minor league teams, improving his game. In 2016, he left the minor leagues and began playing for the New York Yankees.

During Aaron's first full season in 2017, he broke Joe DiMaggio's record for most home runs by a Yankee **rookie**.

Starting in 1933, Joe DiMaggio played with the New York Yankees for 13 years. Here he is at the 1937 All-Star Game.

Fun Facts

The Judge's Chambers is a special cheering section for Aaron Judge at Yankee Stadium. Every home game, fans in the section wear judge's robes and hold up foam **gavels**.

REASONS TO CELEBRATE

While Aaron experienced some injuries for a few years following his first season, there were also reasons to celebrate. One of them was his marriage to Samantha Bracksieck in December 2021.

Fun Facts

In 2019, Aaron created the ALL RISE Foundation. It supports programs and activities that encourage kids to become leaders in their communities.

In 2022, Aaron began setting more records. On September 28, he tied Roger Maris's American League record with his 61st home run of the season.

Aaron celebrates his 61st home run in the seventh inning against the Toronto Blue Jays on September 28, 2022.

Aaron is congratulated by Roger Maris's son after hitting his 61st home run of the season.

When he broke the record with his 62nd home run, Aaron thanked his family, his fans, and his teammates.

Aaron Judge is one of the best players in the American League. Because of his skill and sportsmanship, he has won the respect of his coaches, teammates, and fans.

Aaron speaks to the media on December 21, 2022, when he was introduced as captain of the New York Yankees.

GLOSSARY

agricultural (a-gruh-KUHL-cher-uhl): Having to do with farming

American League (uh-MER-i-kuhn leeg): One of two leagues that make up Major League Baseball

biracial (bye-RAY-shul): Having parents from two races

draft (DRAFT): A process in which sports teams take turns selecting from a group of players

gavel (GA-vuhl): A small wooden hammer used by a judge to get people's attention or call them to order

outfielder (OUT-feel-der): One of three positions on a baseball team that are responsible for getting the ball back to the infield as quickly as possible

professional (pruh-FEH-shuh-nuhl): Someone who is paid to participate in a sport or activity

respect (ri-SPEKT): To admire or look up to someone

rookie (ROOK-ee): A professional athlete in their first season on a team

scholarship (SKOL-er-ship): Money given to a student to pay for their education

scout (SKOUT): A person whose job is to look for talented athletes or performers

INDEX

WEBSITES TO VISIT

https://www.aaronjudgeallrisefoundation.org/

https://www.mlb.com/player/aaron-judge-592450

https://www.mlb.com/news/aaron-judge-breaks-roger-maris-home-run-record-with-62

ABOUT THE AUTHOR

Samantha Bell lives with her family in the foothills of the Blue Ridge Mountains. She has four gray cats with a lot of attitude. When she's not writing, she likes to draw, hike, and visit new places.

Crabtree Publishing

crabtreebooks.com 800-387-7650

Written by: Samantha Bell
Designed by: Kathy Walsh
Series Development: James Earley
Proofreader: Melissa Boyce
Educational Consultant: Marie Lemke M.Ed.
Production manager: Candice Campbell

Hardcover: 978-1-0398-3906-9
Paperback: 978-1-0398-3991-5
Ebook (pdf): 978-1-0398-4063-8
Epub: 978-1-0398-4135-2

Printed in the U.S.A./CP2025

Published in Canada
Crabtree Publishing
616 Welland Ave.
St. Catharines, Ontario
L2M 5V6

Published in the United States
Crabtree Publishing
347 Fifth Ave
Suite 1402-145
New York, NY 10016

Library and Archives Canada Cataloguing in Publication
Available at Library and Archives Canada

Library of Congress Cataloging-in-Publication Data
Available at the Library of Congress

Photographs: Shutterstock, Newscom: Cover, Title pg, Backgrounds: Kyodonews@Newscom, Anna Davidovskaya, StockAppeal, Vector Tradition, Miloje; Background: Anna Davidovskaya; p 5, 14: StockAppeal; p 7, 11, 14, 19, 21, 25: Vector Tradition; p3: Leslie Plaza Johnson/Icon Sports; p 4: Ray Stubblebine; p 5: Corey Sipkin; p 6 & 7: Larry Radloff/ icon Sportswire; p 8: Rich Graessle/Icon SMIv; p 9: Dustin Satloff; p 10: Suzanne Tucker; p 11: Andrew Lahodynskyj; p 12: JoeSAPhotos; p 13: XiXinXing; p 14: Patrick Gorski/ Icon Sportswire; p 15: Anton Garin, Staton Rabin; p 16-19: Josh Holmberg; p 20: Staton Rabin; p 21: Cliff Welch/Icon Sportswire; p 22: @Wiki; p 23: Ron Sachs/CNP/AdMedia, Elsa; p 24: Xavier Collin/Image Press Agency; p 25: Air Images, Suzanne Tucker; p 26, 27: Andrew Lahodynskyj; p 28: Richard B. Levine; p 29: Kyodonews; p 30: John Angelillo